From Broke to Boss - The Ultimate Guide to Success

Michael Ferguson

Published by Michael Ferguson, 2024.

FROM BROKE TO BOSS - THE ULTIMATE GUIDE TO SUCCESS

First edition. July 20, 2024.

ISBN: 979-8227316103

Written by Michael Ferguson.

Introduction

Welcome to the Journey from Broke to Boss

So, you've found yourself broke. Congratulations! You're about to embark on a journey that will not only change your bank balance but also give you stories that will make your friends laugh and maybe, just maybe, help you avoid awkward dinner party silences forever. This book is your guide to navigating the rocky, often hilarious road from financial despair to entrepreneurial triumph. And let's face it: if you're going to be broke, you might as well enjoy the ride.

Before we dive in, let's get one thing straight: this is not your typical self-help book. If you're looking for stiff advice from someone who's never had their lights turned off for non-payment, you've picked the wrong book. Here, we embrace the chaos, laugh at the missteps, and celebrate the small wins with the kind of enthusiasm usually reserved for finding a forgotten $20 bill in your winter coat pocket.

When you're broke, you're in a unique position. You've hit rock bottom, which means there's nowhere to go but up. It's liberating in a way, isn't it? You're free from the burdens of wealth: no high-stress investment decisions, no worrying about losing it all in a bad stock market day, and no pretending to understand what "diversifying your portfolio" means. You, my friend, have the opportunity to build something from the ground up, and this book will be your blueprint.

Why Humor is Your Best Ally

They say laughter is the best medicine, but when you're broke, it's more like the only medicine. Bills piling up? Laugh. Rejected from yet another job? Laugh. Eating ramen for the third time this week? Laugh, and maybe add an egg for variety. Humor is your secret weapon in the battle against financial despair. It keeps you sane, makes you resilient, and turns your journey from broke to boss into a series of hilarious anecdotes rather than a sob story.

Let's face it: navigating the world when you're strapped for cash is challenging. But if you can find the humor in the struggle, you're already a step ahead. Laughter helps you cope with setbacks, keeps you motivated, and attracts people who want to help. So, get ready to laugh your way to success. After all, if you can find joy in the little things—like finding a quarter in the couch cushions—you're on the right path.

The Power of a Knock: Starting with Door-to-Door

Now, let's talk about the power of a knock. I know, I know. Door-to-door sales sounds like something out of a 1950s sitcom, but hear me out. There's a reason this method has stood the test of time. It's personal, direct, and it works. When you're broke, you don't have the luxury of waiting for opportunities to come to you. You need to go out and grab them by the proverbial horns.

Think of door-to-door as your training ground. It's where you'll hone your pitch, develop resilience, and learn to turn rejection into motivation. Plus, it's full of unexpected moments that will keep you laughing. Like the time I knocked on a door and was greeted by a parrot who promptly told me to "go away" before I even had a chance to speak. Or the elderly lady who invited me in for tea, only to spend the next hour trying to sell me her vintage Avon collection. You can't make this stuff up.

Starting with door-to-door sales forces you out of your comfort zone and into the world of hustle. It's not glamorous, but it's effective. And who knows? You might even enjoy it. There's a certain thrill in the unpredictability of it all. One moment you're standing on a stranger's porch, the next you're closing a deal that could change your life.

Embracing the Broke Life

Accepting your financial reality is the first step toward changing it. Denial is not just a river in Egypt; it's a state of mind that keeps you stuck. So let's rip off the Band-Aid and face the facts: you're broke.

And that's okay. We've all been there. Some of us more than once. But acknowledging your situation doesn't mean you have to wallow in it. It means you're ready to do something about it.

When you're broke, every penny counts. And I mean every single one. Remember those couch cushions? They're not just for quarters. I once found a dollar bill stuffed between the cushions and celebrated like I'd won the lottery. Embrace the small victories. They add up. Budgeting when you have no budget is an art form. It's about making the most of what you have, getting creative with your resources, and finding joy in the little things.

The broke life is full of lessons. It teaches you resourcefulness, resilience, and the ability to laugh in the face of adversity. It's easy to find humor in the absurdity of it all. Like the time I made a week's worth of meals out of a can of beans, a bag of rice, and sheer determination. Or the time I turned a thrift store suit into a power outfit that landed me a freelance gig. When you're broke, you become a master of improvisation.

Identifying Your Hustle

Now that we've embraced the broke life, it's time to find your hustle. And here's the thing: your hustle doesn't have to be glamorous. It just has to work. Think about what you're good at, what you enjoy, and what people are willing to pay for. It might be something you've never considered. It might be something you already do as a hobby. The key is to find a way to monetize it.

From hobbies to hustles, the possibilities are endless. Are you a whiz at fixing things? Consider offering handyman services. Great with kids? Babysitting or tutoring could be your ticket. Love animals? Dog walking or pet sitting might be your calling. The point is, everyone has something they can turn into a hustle. And sometimes, it's the most unexpected talents that bring in the most cash.

The art of side gigs is all about juggling multiple incomes. When you're broke, you can't rely on a single source of income. You need to diversify. Think of yourself as a financial juggler, keeping multiple balls in the air at once. It might be exhausting, but it's also exhilarating. And with each new gig, you're building a network, gaining experience, and moving one step closer to your goal.

The Door-to-Door Mindset

Starting with door-to-door sales is more than just a means to an end. It's a mindset. It's about embracing rejection, learning from it, and using it to fuel your drive. It's about developing a thick skin and a winning pitch. It's about turning every knock into an opportunity.

Overcoming the fear of rejection is one of the biggest hurdles you'll face. But here's the secret: rejection isn't personal. It's just part of the process. Every "no" brings you closer to a "yes." And with each rejection, you're learning, growing, and refining your approach. Think of it as a numbers game. The more doors you knock on, the more chances you have to succeed.

Developing a winning pitch is crucial. You need to be confident, concise, and compelling. You need to believe in what you're selling, whether it's a product, a service, or yourself. And most importantly, you need to be able to adapt. Each door is a new opportunity, and each person is a new challenge. Learn to read your audience, tailor your pitch to their needs, and always be ready to pivot.

Turning knocks into opportunities is the ultimate goal. Each door you knock on is a potential gateway to success. It's not just about making a sale; it's about building relationships, creating connections, and planting seeds that might grow into something bigger. Remember, every successful entrepreneur started somewhere. For you, it might be with a knock on a door.

Building Your Business on a Budget

Starting a business when you're broke is no easy feat, but it's not impossible. It's about being resourceful, creative, and determined. DIY marketing is your best friend. Promote yourself for free using social media, word of mouth, and community events. Network with no network by attending local meetups, joining online forums, and reaching out to potential mentors. And don't be afraid to ask for help. You'd be surprised how many people are willing to lend a hand.

The magic of microloans and crowdfunding can't be underestimated. These tools allow you to raise funds without going into debt. Look into platforms like Kickstarter, GoFundMe, and Kiva. Share your story, explain your vision, and rally support. People love to help underdogs, especially when there's a compelling narrative involved.

Scaling up without screwing up is the next challenge. As your business grows, you'll need to hire help, automate processes, and focus on customer retention. Hiring help when you're still broke might seem daunting, but there are ways to do it on a budget. Consider bartering services, offering internships, or partnering with other small businesses. Automating on a shoestring budget means finding affordable tools and software to streamline your operations. And the importance of customer retention can't be overstated. Happy customers are loyal customers, and they'll help spread the word about your business.

Navigating Setbacks with a Smile

Setbacks are inevitable, but they don't have to be devastating. Turning failures into funny stories is a skill that will serve you well. When something goes wrong, find the humor in it. Share your experiences with others, and laugh at the absurdity of it all. The role of resilience in entrepreneurship is crucial. You need to be able to bounce back from setbacks, learn from them, and keep moving forward.

When to pivot is a question every entrepreneur faces at some point. Sometimes, despite your best efforts, things just aren't working. Recognize when it's time to change your business model, and don't be afraid to try something new. Pivoting doesn't mean you've failed; it means you're adaptable and willing to evolve.

Balancing Work and Life

Avoiding burnout when you're your own boss is essential. It's easy to get caught up in the hustle and forget to take care of yourself. Remember to set boundaries, take breaks, and prioritize your well-being. Maintaining relationships while hustling hard can be challenging, but it's important. Make time for family and friends, and don't let your work consume you.

Finding joy in the journey is what it's all about. Celebrate the small wins, laugh at the setbacks, and enjoy the process. Building your business is a marathon, not a sprint. Take it one step at a time, and remember to have fun along the way.

Celebrating Small Wins

Recognizing and rewarding milestones is essential for staying motivated. Celebrate every achievement, no matter how small. Treat yourself to something special, share your success with friends and family, and take pride in how far you've come. Sharing your success with humor and humility is important. People are drawn to authenticity, so don't be afraid to show your true self. Be humble in your achievements and generous in your praise of others.

Planning for long-term success is the ultimate goal. Set realistic goals, stay focused, and keep pushing forward. Remember, the journey from broke to boss is a marathon, not a sprint. Take it one step at a time, and enjoy the ride.

Conclusion

Reflecting on your journey from broke to boss is a rewarding experience. Look back on how far you've come, the challenges you've overcome, and the successes you've achieved. Use this reflection to inspire and motivate you for the future.

Encouragement for future entrepreneurs is crucial. Share your story, offer advice, and be a source of inspiration for others. Remember, you were once in their shoes.

Keeping the humor alive in your business life is essential. Laughter is a powerful tool that can help you navigate the ups and downs of entrepreneurship. So keep laughing, keep hustling, and keep pushing forward. You've got this.

Chapter 1: Are You Broke?

Accepting Your Financial Reality

Alright, let's rip off the Band-Aid and get real: you're broke. Maybe you've been here before, or perhaps this is a new and unsettling experience for you. Either way, accepting your financial reality is the first step toward changing it. It's like facing the monster under your bed; once you shine a light on it, it's not as scary as you thought.

Being broke isn't the end of the world. In fact, it can be the beginning of something beautiful. Think of it as a blank slate. When you have nothing, you have everything to gain. It's an opportunity to rebuild, refocus, and reinvent yourself. But first, you need to come to terms with where you are.

Acknowledging your situation doesn't mean you're admitting defeat. On the contrary, it means you're ready to fight. Denial is a warm, comforting blanket, but it won't keep you warm at night when the heating bill is unpaid. So, toss that blanket aside and embrace the cold, hard truth. You're broke, but you're not broken.

Finding the Funny Side of Being Penniless

When you're broke, the world can seem like a bleak, unforgiving place. But here's the thing: life is absurd, and there's humor in every situation, even the direst ones. Finding the funny side of being penniless isn't about making light of your struggles; it's about finding joy and laughter amidst the chaos.

Consider this: when you're broke, you become a master of improvisation. You learn to make do with what you have, and sometimes, the results are hilarious. Ever tried to cook a gourmet meal with nothing but a can of beans, a pack of ramen, and some questionable spices you found in the back of your cupboard? It's like being on your own personal episode of "Chopped."

Or think about the creative ways you've found to entertain yourself without spending money. I once turned a broken umbrella into an avant-garde piece of yard art. Did it look ridiculous? Absolutely. But it made me laugh every time I saw it, and that laughter was worth more than any store-bought decoration.

Humor is a powerful tool. It helps you cope with stress, builds resilience, and makes life more enjoyable. When you can laugh at your situation, you take away its power to make you feel helpless. So, embrace the absurdity of being broke. Share your funny stories with friends and family. Find joy in the little things, like discovering a hidden talent for thrift store shopping or mastering the art of couponing.

Budgeting When You Have No Budget

Budgeting when you're broke might seem like an oxymoron. How can you budget when there's nothing to budget with? But that's precisely when budgeting becomes most crucial. It's about making the most of what you have, stretching every dollar, and finding creative ways to cut costs.

First, take a hard look at your expenses. Write down everything you spend money on, no matter how small. You'll be surprised at how quickly those little purchases add up. Once you have a clear picture of where your money is going, it's time to prioritize. Separate your needs from your wants. Rent, utilities, and groceries are non-negotiable. That daily latte from the coffee shop? Not so much.

Now, it's time to get creative. How can you reduce your expenses? Can you switch to a cheaper phone plan? Negotiate a lower rate on your internet bill? Cook at home instead of eating out? Every little bit helps. And don't be afraid to think outside the box. I once saved a significant amount on my grocery bill by joining a local food co-op and volunteering a few hours a month in exchange for discounted produce.

Income is the other side of the budgeting equation. If your current income isn't enough to cover your expenses, it's time to find ways to boost it. This might mean picking up a part-time job, freelancing, or starting a side hustle. We'll delve into finding your hustle later in the book, but for now, know that there are plenty of ways to make extra money if you're willing to put in the effort.

Remember, budgeting when you're broke isn't about depriving yourself. It's about making smart choices, being resourceful, and finding joy in the process. It's about taking control of your finances and turning your situation around. And who knows? You might even discover a hidden talent for frugality that will serve you well long after your financial situation improves.

Embracing the Broke Life: A Day in the Life

Let's take a moment to walk through a typical day in the life of someone embracing the broke life. Imagine waking up in the morning with a sense of purpose, ready to tackle the challenges ahead with humor and determination.

Your day starts with a cup of homemade coffee. No fancy lattes here, just good old-fashioned drip coffee brewed in a pot you bought at a yard sale. You sip your coffee while checking your budget for the day. Maybe you've set aside a few dollars for groceries, or perhaps you're planning to hit up a local food pantry later.

After breakfast, it's time to get to work. Maybe you're freelancing, doing odd jobs, or starting your own business. Whatever it is, you approach it with enthusiasm and a sense of humor. When you're broke, every gig, no matter how small, is a step toward financial freedom.

You spend your lunch break getting creative with leftovers. Today's menu? A stir-fry made from last night's veggies and some rice you found in the back of the cupboard. It's not gourmet, but it's delicious, and you take pride in your culinary ingenuity.

In the afternoon, you head out to run errands. You walk instead of driving to save on gas, and you make a game out of finding the best deals. Who knew grocery shopping could be so much fun? You hit up thrift stores, bargain bins, and clearance racks, all while keeping an eye out for hidden treasures.

As the day winds down, you spend some time working on your side hustle. Maybe you're writing a blog, creating art, or selling handmade crafts online. It's a labor of love, and every sale, no matter how small, brings you one step closer to your goals.

In the evening, you unwind with some free entertainment. Maybe you watch a movie from the library, play a board game with friends, or take a walk in the park. You find joy in the simple things, and you end the day with a sense of accomplishment and gratitude.

The Psychology of Being Broke

Let's take a deeper dive into the psychology of being broke. It's easy to feel overwhelmed, stressed, and even ashamed when you're struggling financially. But understanding the mental and emotional aspects of being broke can help you navigate these challenges and come out stronger on the other side.

First, recognize that being broke doesn't define your worth. Society often equates success with financial status, but your value as a person isn't tied to your bank balance. You are more than your financial situation. Remind yourself of your strengths, talents, and achievements. Focus on what you can control and take pride in the steps you're taking to improve your situation.

Next, let's talk about stress. Financial stress is real, and it can take a toll on your mental and physical health. It's important to find healthy ways to cope. Exercise, meditation, and deep breathing can help reduce stress and improve your overall well-being. Find activities that bring you joy and make time for them, even if it's just a few minutes a day.

Support systems are crucial. Don't be afraid to reach out to friends, family, or community resources for help. Talking about your struggles with someone who understands can be incredibly therapeutic. And remember, you're not alone. Many people have been where you are and have come out the other side stronger and more resilient.

Finally, keep a positive mindset. It's easy to get caught up in negative thoughts when you're broke, but focusing on the positive can make a huge difference. Celebrate your small victories, practice gratitude, and remind yourself that this is just a temporary situation. You have the power to change your circumstances and create a better future.

Finding Joy in the Little Things

When you're broke, it's easy to feel like you're missing out on the good things in life. But the truth is, joy can be found in the simplest of pleasures. It's about shifting your perspective and appreciating what you have, rather than focusing on what you lack.

Take a moment to reflect on the things that bring you joy. Maybe it's spending time with loved ones, enjoying a beautiful sunset, or savoring a delicious meal. These moments don't cost anything, but they're priceless. Make a conscious effort to seek out and savor these simple pleasures.

Gratitude is another powerful tool. When you focus on what you're grateful for, it's hard to stay negative. Start a gratitude journal and write down three things you're thankful for each day. They don't have to be big things; it could be something as simple as a warm cup of tea or a kind word from a friend.

Finding joy in the little things is about being present and mindful. It's about slowing down and appreciating the beauty in everyday moments. When you embrace this mindset, you'll find that even the most mundane tasks can bring a sense of fulfillment and happiness.

The Community of the Broke

One of the surprising benefits of being broke is the sense of community it can create. When you're struggling, you often find that you're not alone. There are others in similar situations, and together, you can support and uplift each other.

Building a community of the broke is about connecting with others who understand what you're going through. It's about sharing resources, offering encouragement, and celebrating each other's successes. This community can take many forms, from online support groups to local meetups.

In a community of the broke, everyone looks out for each other. Maybe you share tips on finding the best deals, swap skills and services, or simply lend a listening ear when someone needs to vent. This sense of camaraderie can make a huge difference in your journey from broke to boss.

So, seek out your community. Look for people who are on the same path as you and build relationships based on mutual support and understanding. Together, you can overcome the challenges of being broke and celebrate the triumphs along the way.

Humor as a Survival Tool

Humor is more than just a way to pass the time; it's a survival tool. When you're broke, laughter can be a lifeline. It lightens the mood, reduces stress, and helps you see your situation in a new light.

Think of humor as a pressure valve. When things get tough, a good laugh can release the tension and make everything feel a little more manageable. It's a way to take a step back and find perspective, to see the absurdity in your struggles and realize that, in the grand scheme of things, it's not the end of the world.

Incorporate humor into your daily life. Watch funny movies, read humorous books, or follow comedians on social media. Surround yourself with people who make you laugh and find ways to bring humor into your interactions. Even in the darkest times, there's always something to laugh about if you look hard enough.

Conclusion

Embracing the broke life is about more than just surviving; it's about thriving. It's about finding joy in the journey, building a community of support, and using humor as a tool to navigate the ups and downs. When you accept your financial reality, find the funny side of being penniless, and learn to budget creatively, you're setting the stage for a brighter future.

So, take a deep breath and dive in. This journey from broke to boss won't be easy, but it will be worth it. Embrace the challenges, celebrate the victories, and remember to laugh along the way. You've got this.

Chapter 2: Embracing the Broke Life

Accepting Your Financial Reality

When you're broke and have three single children relying on you, it can feel like the weight of the world is on your shoulders. Accepting your financial reality is not just about facing facts; it's about making peace with where you are so you can plan where you're going.

I remember a time when my bank account balance was so low that I could practically see the bottom of the barrel. I was living in a cramped apartment with my three kids, juggling between their needs and my futile attempts to stretch every penny. Acceptance didn't come easy, but it was necessary. Every parent wants to shield their children from hardships, but acknowledging that we were broke was the first step towards change.

It's essential to look at your situation squarely and say, "This is where we are, but it's not where we're staying." Acceptance isn't synonymous with defeat. Rather, it's about understanding the present so you can pave the way for a better future. It's about being honest with yourself and your children about your circumstances while instilling hope and determination.

Finding the Funny Side of Being Penniless

Life is absurd, and there's always something to laugh about, even when times are tough. I remember one particularly challenging month when we were down to the last roll of toilet paper. My youngest, ever the curious one, asked why we couldn't buy more. "Well," I said, "we're on a budget, and it's a tight squeeze." We all laughed, even though it was more out of necessity than genuine humor.

Finding the funny side of being penniless doesn't mean ignoring the seriousness of your situation; it's about lifting your spirits and finding light in the darkness. Like the time when our old car broke down, and we had to take the bus everywhere. The kids turned it into an adventure, pretending we were on a grand tour of the city. Their laughter and imaginative games made those bus rides some of our most memorable moments.

Humor can also diffuse tension. When you're feeling overwhelmed, a good laugh can break the ice and bring everyone together. I once attempted to make homemade bread to save money. It turned out to be more of a rock than a loaf. We had a good laugh about it, named it "Breadzilla," and it became a running joke in our family. Moments like these remind us that even in hardship, joy can be found.

Budgeting When You Have No Budget

Budgeting when you're broke with three children to care for feels like trying to squeeze water from a stone. It's a daunting task, but it's also where creativity and resourcefulness come into play. Every penny counts, and it's about making each one stretch as far as possible.

The first step is to write down every expense, no matter how small. You'd be surprised how quickly those seemingly insignificant purchases add up. I once realized we were spending a significant chunk on snacks. Cutting back on pre-packaged treats and making homemade snacks not only saved money but also became a fun activity with the kids.

Next, prioritize your spending. Rent, utilities, and groceries are non-negotiable. But for everything else, it's about asking, "Do we need this, or can we make do without it?" One winter, instead of buying new coats, we patched up the old ones and added layers underneath. It wasn't glamorous, but it kept us warm.

When it comes to groceries, meal planning is your best friend. Planning meals for the week helps avoid impulse buys and ensures nothing goes to waste. I learned to get creative with leftovers, turning Sunday's roast chicken into Monday's chicken soup and Tuesday's chicken salad. It became a game to see how far we could stretch one meal into multiple dishes.

Income is another critical aspect. If your current income isn't enough, look for ways to supplement it. I took on freelance writing jobs in the evenings after the kids were in bed. It wasn't easy, but every little bit helped. We'll explore finding your hustle in more detail later, but for now, know that there are ways to earn extra income if you're willing to put in the effort.

Stories from the Broke Life

Let's take a deeper dive into some stories from my time navigating the broke life with three single children and no support. These stories are a testament to resilience, creativity, and the power of laughter.

The Power of Pancakes

There was a time when our pantry was practically empty, and I had to make breakfast for the kids. I found some flour, a bit of milk, and an egg. Pancakes it was. The problem was, we didn't have any syrup. I scoured the cupboards and found an old jar of honey, but it was crystallized.

Undeterred, I heated it up, but it didn't quite liquefy as expected. The kids watched as I tried to pour the thick, gooey mess onto their pancakes. We ended up with a mound of pancake pieces stuck together with what we called "honey glue." It was a disaster, but the kids found it hilarious. We laughed, dubbed them "sticky pancakes," and made a game out of trying to eat them without getting stuck. That morning, our empty pantry turned into a memorable bonding moment.

The Great Christmas Miracle

Christmas is a challenging time when you're broke. One year, I had no idea how I was going to afford presents for the kids. I decided to get creative and make gifts. I found some old fabric scraps and sewed stuffed animals for them. They weren't perfect, but they were made with love.

On Christmas morning, the kids opened their handmade gifts. Their faces lit up with joy, not because the toys were fancy, but because they appreciated the effort and love that went into making them. Later that day, a neighbor surprised us with a basket of treats and small toys for the kids. It felt like a Christmas miracle, reminding us that kindness and generosity exist even in tough times.

The Coin Jar Adventure

There was a time when we were down to our last few dollars, and I needed to buy groceries. I remembered an old coin jar we had been collecting spare change in. I dumped it out on the table, and the kids and I sorted through the coins, counting every penny. It turned into a fun math lesson for them and a way to scrape together enough money for essentials.

We walked to the grocery store, our pockets jangling with coins. The cashier's eyes widened when we paid for our items with a pile of change, but she was patient and kind. We left the store with a sense of accomplishment, having turned a dire situation into an adventure. That coin jar saved us more times than I can count, proving that even the smallest savings can make a difference.

Embracing the Chaos

Life with three kids is always chaotic, but when you're broke, that chaos takes on a new level. It's about finding ways to manage the madness and finding peace amidst the pandemonium.

One summer, the kids were off school, and I couldn't afford summer camps or activities. Instead, we made the most of what we had. We turned our tiny backyard into a camping site, complete with a makeshift tent made from old sheets. We roasted marshmallows over a small fire pit and told stories under the stars. It wasn't a fancy vacation, but it was one of the best summers we ever had.

Another time, during a particularly rough patch, I couldn't afford new school supplies. We gathered all the leftover supplies from the previous year and got creative. The kids decorated their old notebooks with stickers and drawings, turning them into personalized works of art. They were proud of their creations, and I was proud of their resilience and creativity.

The Community of the Broke

Being broke can feel isolating, but it's also an opportunity to build a sense of community. I found that there were others in similar situations, and together, we supported each other.

I joined a local group of single parents who were also struggling financially. We shared tips, resources, and most importantly, a sense of solidarity. We organized potluck dinners, where everyone brought what they could, and we shared meals and stories. It was a way to lighten the load and remind ourselves that we weren't alone.

One particularly memorable experience was when my neighbor, also a single parent, and I decided to swap skills. She was a fantastic seamstress, and I had some experience with home repairs. She helped mend our clothes, and I fixed a leaky faucet in her kitchen. It was a win-win situation and a testament to the power of community.

The Psychology of Being Broke

The psychological impact of being broke can be profound. It's easy to feel overwhelmed, stressed, and even ashamed. But understanding the mental and emotional aspects of being broke can help you navigate these challenges.

First, it's essential to recognize that being broke doesn't define your worth. Society often equates success with financial status, but your value as a person isn't tied to your bank balance. You are more than your financial situation. Remind yourself of your strengths, talents, and achievements. Focus on what you can control and take pride in the steps you're taking to improve your situation.

Next, let's talk about stress. Financial stress is real, and it can take a toll on your mental and physical health. It's important to find healthy ways to cope. Exercise, meditation, and deep breathing can help reduce stress and improve your overall well-being. Find activities that bring you joy and make time for them, even if it's just a few minutes a day.

Support systems are crucial. Don't be afraid to reach out to friends, family, or community resources for help. Talking about your struggles with someone who understands can be incredibly therapeutic. And remember, you're not alone. Many people have been where you are and have come out the other side stronger and more resilient.

Conclusion

Embracing the broke life is about accepting your financial reality, finding humour in the hardships, and learning to budget creatively. It's about building a sense of community, turning challenges into adventures, and maintaining a positive mindset.

Life may be tough, but you are tougher. You have the strength, creativity, and resilience to navigate this journey. Embrace the chaos, laugh at the absurdity, and remember that being broke is just a chapter in your story, not the whole book. Keep moving forward, and know that brighter days are ahead.

Chapter 3: Identifying Your Hustle

Finding Your Passion in the Strangest Places

In the journey from broke to boss, identifying your hustle is crucial. It's not just about finding any job or source of income; it's about discovering what you're passionate about and turning that into a sustainable business. Passion fuels persistence, and persistence leads to success.

The Unexpected Art of Balloon Animals

My journey in identifying my hustle began in the most unexpected place: a children's birthday party. I was desperately in need of extra income, and a friend suggested I help out at her kid's party. She handed me a bag of balloons and a pump, and with a bit of practice and a lot of YouTube tutorials, I became a balloon animal artist.

It wasn't glamorous, and I certainly never imagined myself doing this, but I found joy in it. The kids' faces lit up with every balloon creation, and I realized that this quirky skill could be my ticket to extra income. I started offering my services at other parties and events, and before I knew it, I had a side hustle that not only paid the bills but also brought smiles to countless children.

Turning Struggles into Solutions

Sometimes, your passion is born out of your own struggles. During a particularly tough winter, our heating system broke down. With no money for repairs, I had to get creative to keep my family warm. I discovered the art of making homemade heating pads with rice and old socks. Not only did they work, but they also became a fun project with the kids.

Seeing the potential, I started making these heating pads to sell at local markets. It was a simple solution to a common problem, and people loved them. This experience taught me that our challenges can often lead to innovative solutions, which can then be turned into profitable ventures.

The Power of Listening

Identifying your hustle sometimes comes from listening to others. People often express their needs and frustrations, and if you pay attention, you can find opportunities to help. One day, a neighbor complained about how difficult it was to find reliable pet sitters. As a pet lover myself, I saw an opportunity. I offered to pet sit for her, and word quickly spread. Soon, I had a small but steady stream of clients who trusted me with their furry friends.

By listening to those around you, you can uncover niches that might otherwise go unnoticed. Your hustle doesn't have to be something groundbreaking; it just needs to fulfill a need.

From Hobbies to Hustles: Making Money from What You Love

Turning hobbies into hustles is a dream for many, but it's entirely possible with the right approach. Here's how to take what you love and transform it into a source of income.

Crafting Your Way to Cash

One of my hobbies was making handcrafted jewelry. I enjoyed the process of designing and creating unique pieces, but it never occurred to me that it could be a viable business. One day, I decided to sell a few pieces at a local craft fair. The response was overwhelming. People loved my designs, and I realized that there was a market for my hobby.

I started small, selling at local fairs and online through platforms like Etsy. With each sale, my confidence grew, and so did my business. What began as a simple hobby turned into a profitable hustle that not only provided extra income but also allowed me to do something I loved.

Baking Up a Storm

Another hobby-turned-hustle was baking. My kids and I loved experimenting in the kitchen, creating all sorts of treats. During a particularly tight financial period, I decided to bake a batch of cookies and sell them at a community event. They were a hit.

Encouraged by the response, I began taking orders from friends and neighbors. Birthdays, holidays, and special occasions all became opportunities to showcase my baking skills. I even started offering custom cakes and catering for small events. Baking went from a fun pastime to a reliable source of income, all while allowing me to spend quality time with my kids in the kitchen.

Leveraging Online Platforms

In today's digital age, turning hobbies into hustles has never been easier. Platforms like YouTube, TikTok, and Instagram provide incredible opportunities to showcase your talents and reach a wider audience. I started a YouTube channel where I shared DIY projects, cooking tutorials, and parenting tips. It was a way to connect with others and share my passions.

Over time, the channel gained a following, and I was able to monetize it through ads and sponsorships. What started as a hobby of creating and sharing videos became a significant part of my income. The key is to find what you love, share it with the world, and be consistent.

The Art of Side Gigs: Juggling Multiple Incomes

When you're broke, relying on a single source of income might not be enough. Side gigs can provide the extra financial boost you need. Here's how to juggle multiple incomes without losing your sanity.

Freelance Writing and Editing

One of my first side gigs was freelance writing. With a background in writing and a passion for storytelling, I began offering my services on platforms like Upwork and Fiverr. I wrote articles, blog posts, and even edited manuscripts. It was flexible work that I could do from home, allowing me to balance my responsibilities as a single parent.

Freelance writing opened doors to new opportunities and connections. I built a portfolio, gained repeat clients, and even had the chance to write for some well-known publications. It wasn't always steady work, but it provided a crucial supplementary income.

Ride-Sharing and Delivery Services

For those with reliable transportation, ride-sharing and delivery services can be a flexible and lucrative side gig. I signed up with Uber and DoorDash, driving and delivering food during my free hours. It wasn't glamorous, but it paid the bills and allowed me to work around my children's schedules.

These gigs also provided a chance to meet new people and learn more about my community. I discovered hidden gems in my city, from local restaurants to scenic routes. It was an adventure in itself, and the extra income made a significant difference.

Teaching and Tutoring

Leveraging my skills and knowledge, I started offering tutoring services in subjects I excelled at. Whether it was helping high school students with math or teaching English as a second language, tutoring became a reliable side gig. I used online platforms to connect with students and offered both in-person and virtual sessions.

Teaching and tutoring not only provided income but also a sense of fulfillment. Seeing my students succeed and knowing I played a part in their academic growth was incredibly rewarding.

Balancing Act

Juggling multiple side gigs requires careful planning and time management. I kept a detailed calendar and prioritized tasks based on deadlines and importance. It was a constant balancing act, but with determination and organization, I managed to make it work.

The key to successful juggling is to be flexible and adaptable. Some weeks, one gig might demand more attention, while others take a backseat. It's about finding a rhythm and staying committed to your goals.

Stories of Hustle and Hope

The Art of Multi-Tasking

One particularly busy week, I had freelance writing deadlines, baking orders to fulfill, and tutoring sessions lined up. My kitchen turned into a makeshift bakery, with flour covering every surface and the sweet aroma of cookies filling the air. I had my laptop set up on the counter, typing away between batches.

It was chaotic, but I thrived in that chaos. My kids were my little helpers, mixing dough and decorating cookies. We turned it into a game, and their laughter filled the room. Despite the madness, we made it work. Every task completed, every order fulfilled, and every client satisfied was a step towards financial stability.

From Trash to Treasure

One summer, I noticed a trend of people discarding old furniture on the curb. With a bit of creativity and elbow grease, I saw potential in these abandoned pieces. I started collecting, refurbishing, and selling them. What was once considered trash became beautiful, functional furniture.

I learned to sand, paint, and upholster, transforming each piece into something unique. The process was therapeutic, and the profits were rewarding. It taught me that opportunities are everywhere if you're willing to see them.

The Side Gig that Stuck

Of all the side gigs I tried, freelance writing was the one that stuck. It provided a steady stream of income and allowed me to hone my skills. I eventually expanded my services to include content marketing and social media management, building a small but thriving business.

Freelance writing became more than just a side gig; it became a career. It offered the flexibility I needed as a single parent and the financial stability to support my family. It was proof that with persistence and passion, a side gig can turn into a full-fledged business.

Conclusion

Identifying your hustle is about finding what you're passionate about and turning it into a source of income. It's about leveraging your skills, hobbies, and creativity to create multiple streams of revenue. From balloon animals to baking, and freelance writing to ride-sharing, the possibilities are endless.

The journey from broke to boss is filled with challenges and opportunities. Embrace the hustle, be open to new experiences, and never underestimate the power of a side gig. With determination, creativity, and a bit of humor, you can turn your passions into profits and pave the way to financial independence.

Chapter 4: The Door-to-Door Mindset

Overcoming the Fear of Rejection

Knock, knock. Who's there? Your dreams of financial independence. But first, you must face one of the greatest fears known to humankind: rejection. The fear of rejection can be paralyzing, but in the door-to-door game, it's just another step on the path to success.

Understanding Rejection

Rejection is a natural part of life. From the playground to the professional world, we all experience it. But when you're going door-to-door, rejection feels personal. You're face-to-face with someone who has the power to accept or deny your pitch. This can be daunting, but understanding the nature of rejection can help you overcome it.

Rejection is not a reflection of your worth. It's often about the person's circumstances, mood, or preferences. It's essential to remember that a "no" today doesn't mean a "no" forever. Sometimes, it's just a "not right now."

Building Resilience

Resilience is your greatest ally in the face of rejection. It's the ability to bounce back, learn from the experience, and keep going. Building resilience starts with changing your mindset. Instead of seeing rejection as a failure, view it as a learning opportunity.

Here are some strategies to build resilience:

- **Practice Self-Compassion**: Be kind to yourself. Acknowledge your efforts and remind yourself that everyone faces rejection.

- **Learn from Feedback**: If possible, ask for feedback when you're rejected. It can provide valuable insights to improve your approach.

- **Stay Positive**: Focus on the positives. Celebrate small victories and progress, no matter how minor they seem.

- **Set Realistic Goals**: Break down your goals into manageable steps. Achieving small milestones can boost your confidence and keep you motivated.

The Rejection Game

Turning rejection into a game can make the experience less intimidating. Set a goal for how many rejections you'll aim for in a day. It might sound counterintuitive, but it shifts your focus from the fear of rejection to the act of reaching out.

For example, aim for ten rejections a day. Each rejection brings you closer to your goal and reduces the emotional impact. You'll start to see rejection as a natural part of the process rather than a personal failure.

Developing a Winning Pitch

A great pitch is the cornerstone of successful door-to-door selling. It's your opportunity to make a positive first impression and connect with potential customers. Here's how to craft and deliver a winning pitch.

Know Your Audience

Understanding your audience is crucial. Who are they? What are their needs and pain points? Tailor your pitch to address these needs directly. Research the neighborhood or demographic you're targeting. The more you know about your audience, the more effectively you can engage them. ·

Crafting the Pitch

A winning pitch has several key components:

- **Introduction**: Start with a friendly and confident greeting. Introduce yourself and your purpose.

- **Value Proposition**: Clearly state the benefits of what you're offering. How does it solve a problem or improve their life?

- **Storytelling**: Use a brief story to illustrate the value of your product or service. Stories are memorable and relatable.

- **Call to Action**: End with a clear and compelling call to action. What do you want them to do next? Make it easy for them to take that step.

Practice Makes Perfect

Practice your pitch until it feels natural. Rehearse in front of a mirror, record yourself, or practice with a friend. The more you practice, the more confident you'll become. Pay attention to your tone, body language, and pacing. Confidence is contagious, and a well-delivered pitch can make all the difference.

Adapting on the Fly

No two interactions are the same, so be prepared to adapt your pitch based on the person you're speaking to. Listen actively and respond to their cues. If they express a specific concern, address it directly. Flexibility and adaptability show that you're attentive and genuinely interested in their needs.

Turning Knocks into Opportunities

Every knock on a door is an opportunity, even if it doesn't lead to an immediate sale. It's about building connections, gaining insights, and leaving a positive impression. Here's how to turn each knock into an opportunity.

Building Relationships

Approach each interaction with the goal of building a relationship rather than making a sale. Be genuine, friendly, and respectful. People are more likely to do business with someone they trust and feel comfortable with.

Follow up on conversations, even if they didn't result in a sale. Send a thank-you note or check in to see if their circumstances have changed. Building a rapport can lead to future opportunities and referrals.

Learning from Each Interaction

Each door you knock on is a chance to learn and improve. Pay attention to the responses you receive and adjust your approach accordingly. Keep a journal of your interactions, noting what worked and what didn't. Over time, you'll develop a deeper understanding of your audience and refine your pitch.

Leveraging Referrals

Satisfied customers can be your best advocates. Ask for referrals and provide incentives for them. Word-of-mouth is powerful, and a recommendation from a trusted source can open doors you didn't even know existed.

Expanding Your Network

Every person you meet has a network of their own. Take advantage of this by attending local events, joining community groups, and participating in neighborhood activities. The more people you connect with, the more opportunities you'll uncover.

Stories of Success and Setbacks

The Door That Opened More Doors

One hot summer afternoon, I knocked on a door in a quiet neighborhood. An elderly woman answered, and we struck up a conversation. She wasn't interested in my pitch, but we chatted for a while about her garden and her family. Before I left, she mentioned that her son was looking for someone to help with some home repairs.

I followed up on that lead, and it turned into a steady stream of work. That one conversation opened multiple doors, leading to new clients and referrals. It was a reminder that every knock has the potential to lead to something valuable.

The Lessons from Rejection

Not every knock will be successful, but each one teaches you something. One day, I faced a particularly tough string of rejections. Every door seemed to slam shut in my face. It was discouraging, but I took it as an opportunity to refine my pitch and approach.

I reviewed my interactions, identified common objections, and adjusted my strategy. The next day, I approached the doors with renewed confidence and a revised pitch. The results were noticeably better. Each rejection was a stepping stone to improvement.

The Power of Persistence

Persistence is key in the door-to-door game. There was a neighborhood where I faced consistent rejection. It would have been easy to give up, but I kept going back, refining my approach each time. Eventually, my persistence paid off. I made a connection with a local business owner who needed my services and referred me to others.

Persistence showed that I was serious and committed. It built trust and demonstrated my determination. Over time, that neighborhood became one of my most profitable areas.

Conclusion

The door-to-door mindset is about overcoming the fear of rejection, developing a winning pitch, and turning each knock into an opportunity. It's a journey of resilience, adaptability, and persistence. By embracing these principles, you can turn door-to-door selling into a successful and rewarding endeavor.

Remember, every knock is a chance to connect, learn, and grow. Approach each door with confidence, build genuine relationships, and never underestimate the power of persistence. With the right mindset and strategies, you can turn rejection into opportunity and pave the way to financial independence.

Chapter 5: Building Your Business on a Budget

Starting a business on a tight budget is both a challenge and an opportunity. It forces you to be creative, resourceful, and strategic. In this chapter, we'll explore how to build your business without breaking the bank. We'll cover DIY marketing, networking strategies, and the benefits of microloans and crowdfunding. Prepare to dive into practical strategies that will help you build a solid foundation for your business while keeping costs low.

DIY Marketing: Promoting Yourself for Free

Marketing is essential to building your business, but it doesn't have to be expensive. With a bit of creativity and effort, you can effectively promote yourself and your brand without spending a fortune.

Creating a Strong Online Presence

Your online presence is crucial for attracting and engaging customers. Here's how to establish and grow your digital footprint on a budget:

- **Build a Website**: Platforms like WordPress, Wix, and Squarespace offer free or low-cost website-building options. Choose a clean, professional design that represents your brand well. Even a simple, well-maintained website can make a significant impact.

- **Optimize for Search Engines**: Search engine optimization (SEO) helps your website rank higher in search results. Focus on using relevant keywords, creating quality content, and optimizing your site's structure. Many free tools and guides are available to help you improve your SEO.

- **Utilize Social Media**: Social media platforms like Facebook, Instagram, LinkedIn, and Twitter are free to use and can be powerful tools for marketing. Create profiles for your business and regularly post engaging content. Use hashtags, join relevant groups, and interact with your audience to build a following.

- **Leverage Content Marketing**: Content marketing involves creating and sharing valuable content to attract and retain customers. Start a blog, create informative videos, or develop infographics related to your industry. Share your content on social media and other online platforms to drive traffic to your website.

- **Engage in Online Communities**: Join online forums, groups, and communities related to your industry. Participate in discussions, offer valuable advice, and subtly promote your business. Building relationships in these communities can lead to valuable referrals and partnerships.

Building a Brand Identity

Your brand identity sets you apart from competitors and helps customers recognize and remember you. Here's how to build a strong brand identity on a budget:

- **Design a Logo**: A professional logo is a key element of your brand identity. Use free or low-cost design tools like Canva or LogoMaker to create a logo that reflects your brand's personality and values.

- **Develop a Consistent Style**: Consistency is crucial for brand recognition. Choose a color scheme, font, and visual style that you'll use across all your marketing materials. This consistency helps build trust and familiarity with your audience.

- **Create Business Cards and Flyers**: Even on a budget, you can create effective promotional materials. Design business cards, flyers, and other print materials using free design tools and order them from affordable printing services. Hand them out at events, networking meetings, and in your local community.

Networking with No Network

Networking is essential for building relationships, finding opportunities, and growing your business. If you're starting with a limited network, don't worry. There are plenty of ways to build connections and expand your reach.

Attending Local Events

Local events, such as business expos, community fairs, and networking mixers, are great opportunities to meet potential customers, partners, and mentors. Even if you're on a tight budget, you can often find free or low-cost events to attend.

- **Research Local Events**: Look for local events related to your industry or business interests. Check community bulletin boards, social media groups, and event listings for opportunities to connect with others.

- **Prepare Your Elevator Pitch**: Before attending events, prepare a concise and compelling elevator pitch. This pitch should briefly explain who you are, what your business does, and what sets you apart.

- **Follow Up**: After meeting new contacts, follow up with a thank-you note or email. Stay in touch by sharing valuable information, offering support, or simply checking in periodically.

Leveraging Online Networking

Online networking can be just as effective as in-person networking. Use online platforms to connect with others in your industry and build valuable relationships.

- **Join Professional Groups**: LinkedIn groups, industry-specific forums, and online communities are great places to connect with like-minded professionals. Participate in discussions, share your expertise, and build relationships with other members.

- **Engage on Social Media**: Follow industry leaders, influencers, and potential customers on social media. Engage with their content by liking, commenting, and sharing. This can help you build visibility and establish connections.

- **Offer Value**: Share valuable content, advice, and insights with your network. Offering value without expecting anything in return can help you build credibility and attract opportunities.

Building Relationships with Mentors

Finding a mentor can provide valuable guidance, support, and connections. Here's how to find and build relationships with mentors:

- **Identify Potential Mentors**: Look for individuals in your industry who have experience and expertise that align with your goals. Reach out to them with a personalized message expressing your admiration and interest in learning from them.

- **Offer to Help**: When approaching potential mentors, offer something of value in return. This could be assistance with a project, sharing your own expertise, or helping with tasks they might need support with.

- **Be Respectful of Their Time**: Mentors are often busy professionals. Be respectful of their time and approach them with clear, specific questions or requests. Show appreciation for their guidance and maintain a professional demeanor.

The Magic of Microloans and Crowdfunding

When starting a business on a budget, traditional financing options might be out of reach. However, microloans and crowdfunding offer alternative ways to secure the funds you need.

Microloans

Microloans are small loans designed to support small businesses and entrepreneurs. They're often offered by non-profit organizations, community lenders, and online platforms.

- **Research Microloan Providers**: Look for organizations that offer microloans in your area or industry. Organizations like Kiva, Accion, and the Small Business Administration (SBA) provide microloans to entrepreneurs with limited access to traditional financing.

- **Prepare Your Application**: When applying for a microloan, be prepared to provide a detailed business plan, financial projections, and information about your personal and business background. A well-prepared application increases your chances of approval.

- **Understand the Terms**: Carefully review the terms and conditions of any microloan you're considering. Pay attention to interest rates, repayment schedules, and any fees or penalties.

Crowdfunding

Crowdfunding allows you to raise funds from a large number of people, typically through online platforms. It's a great way to secure financing while also building a customer base and generating buzz for your business.

- **Choose a Crowdfunding Platform**: Platforms like Kickstarter, Indiegogo, and GoFundMe offer different types of crowdfunding options. Research each platform to find one that aligns with your business goals and needs.

- **Create a Compelling Campaign**: A successful crowdfunding campaign requires a compelling story and a clear value proposition. Create a detailed and engaging campaign page that explains your business, your goals, and what you're offering in return for contributions.

- **Promote Your Campaign**: Once your campaign is live, promote it through social media, email, and other marketing channels. Engage with your backers, provide regular updates, and express gratitude for their support.

- **Deliver on Promises**: If your campaign is successful, ensure that you deliver on your promises to backers. Fulfill rewards, provide updates, and maintain transparency throughout the process.

Case Studies of Budget-Friendly Success

The Bootstrapper's Journey

One entrepreneur started with nothing more than a small savings account and a big idea. She used free online resources to create a website, designed her own marketing materials, and relied on social media to spread the word about her business. By leveraging local networking events and online communities, she built a loyal customer base. Her resourcefulness and determination led to a successful business with minimal upfront costs.

'The Crowdfunding Success Story

A startup sought to develop a new product but lacked the capital to get started. They turned to crowdfunding, creating a compelling campaign that showcased their innovative product and its potential benefits. Through targeted social media promotion and engaging content, they raised enough funds to launch their product and gain valuable customer feedback. The crowdfunding campaign not only provided the necessary capital but also helped build a dedicated customer base.

'The Microloan Game-Changer

A small business owner needed funds to expand their operations but faced difficulties securing traditional financing. They applied for a microloan from a community lender, providing a detailed business plan and financial projections. The loan enabled them to invest in new equipment and hire additional staff, leading to increased revenue and growth. The microloan proved to be a crucial step in their business journey.

Conclusion

Building a business on a budget is a challenge, but it's also an opportunity to be creative, resourceful, and strategic. By leveraging DIY marketing, networking effectively, and exploring alternative financing options like microloans and crowdfunding, you can lay a strong foundation for your business without breaking the bank.

Embrace the constraints of your budget as a driving force for innovation and ingenuity. With the right mindset and strategies, you can turn financial limitations into a springboard for success. Stay focused, be persistent, and remember that every great business started with a small investment and a big idea.

Chapter 6: Scaling Up Without Screwing Up

Scaling a business is both an exciting and daunting task. As you transition from a startup to a growing enterprise, you'll face new challenges and opportunities. This chapter will guide you through scaling up while maintaining control over your resources and operations. We'll cover hiring help when you're still broke, automating on a shoestring budget, and the importance of customer retention. Prepare to delve into strategies and tips that will help you expand your business efficiently and effectively.

Hiring Help When You're Still Broke

Hiring employees can be a significant expense, but as your business grows, you may need additional help to manage increased workloads and responsibilities. Here's how to approach hiring without breaking the bank.

Assessing Your Needs

Before hiring, evaluate your business needs and identify the roles that will have the most impact. Consider the following steps:

- **Identify Key Areas for Support**: Determine which aspects of your business are consuming the most time or causing bottlenecks. Focus on hiring for roles that will alleviate these pressures and contribute to growth.

- **Prioritize Tasks**: Make a list of tasks that need to be handled and prioritize them. This will help you decide which positions are most critical and what skills are required.

- **Consider Part-Time or Freelance Help**: If full-time employees are not feasible, consider part-time or freelance workers. They can provide the necessary support without the long-term commitment and expense of full-time hires.

Finding the Right Talent

Finding the right people to join your team can make a huge difference. Here are some tips for hiring effectively:

- **Utilize Free Job Boards**: Use free job boards and platforms like Indeed, LinkedIn, and Glassdoor to post job openings. You can also tap into local community boards and online forums.

- **Leverage Your Network**: Reach out to your network for recommendations. Sometimes, the best candidates come from personal referrals.

- **Offer Internships**: Offering internships can provide you with additional help while giving students or recent graduates valuable experience. Ensure that the internship is mutually beneficial and provides a learning opportunity.

- **Consider Equity Compensation**: For key positions, offering equity or profit-sharing can be an attractive alternative to a high salary. It aligns the interests of your team with the success of the business.

Managing Your Team Efficiently

Once you've hired help, managing them effectively is crucial:

- **Set Clear Expectations**: Communicate your expectations clearly from the start. Define roles, responsibilities, and performance metrics.

- **Provide Training**: Invest time in training your team to ensure they understand your business processes and values. Well-trained employees are more productive and aligned with your goals.

- **Foster a Positive Culture**: Create a positive work environment that encourages collaboration, growth, and open communication. A motivated and engaged team is more likely to contribute to your business's success.

Automating on a Shoestring Budget

Automation can significantly improve efficiency and save time, but it doesn't have to be expensive. Implementing cost-effective automation solutions can streamline your operations and reduce manual work.

Identifying Automation Opportunities

Evaluate your business processes to identify areas where automation can be implemented. Consider automating the following:

- **Marketing**: Use email marketing platforms like Mailchimp or Sendinblue to automate email campaigns. Schedule social media posts using tools like Buffer or Hootsuite.

- **Customer Service**: Implement chatbots on your website to handle common customer inquiries. Many affordable or free chatbot platforms can integrate with your existing systems.

- **Accounting and Invoicing**: Utilize accounting software like Wave or QuickBooks to automate invoicing, expense tracking, and financial reporting.

- **Order Fulfillment**: If you sell products online, consider using fulfillment services that automate order processing and shipping. Look for affordable options that scale with your business.

Choosing Affordable Tools and Platforms

There are many budget-friendly tools available to help with automation:

- **Zapier**: Zapier connects different apps and automates workflows between them. It offers a free plan with basic automation features and affordable pricing for advanced plans.

- **Google Workspace**: Google Workspace (formerly G Suite) provides tools like Google Sheets, Docs, and Drive that can be used to automate and streamline various business processes.

- **Trello and Asana**: These project management tools help automate task management and team collaboration. Both offer free versions with essential features.

Implementing and Testing Automation

When implementing automation:

- **Start Small**: Begin with one or two processes to automate and gradually expand. This allows you to test and refine your automation strategy without overwhelming your systems.

- **Monitor Performance**: Regularly review the performance of your automated processes. Ensure they are functioning as intended and making a positive impact on your business.

- **Adjust as Needed**: Be prepared to make adjustments based on performance and feedback. Automation should enhance your operations, not create new problems.

The Importance of Customer Retention

Customer retention is crucial for sustainable growth. It's often more cost-effective to retain existing customers than to acquire new ones. Building strong relationships with your customers can lead to repeat business, referrals, and long-term success.

Building Strong Customer Relationships

Developing strong relationships with your customers involves:

- **Providing Exceptional Service**: Ensure that every customer interaction is positive. Train your team to be responsive, helpful, and courteous.

- **Personalizing Communication**: Use customer data to personalize communication and offers. Address customers by name and tailor your messages to their preferences and behaviors.

- **Soliciting Feedback**: Regularly seek feedback from your customers to understand their needs and expectations. Use surveys, reviews, and direct communication to gather insights.

Implementing Loyalty Programs

Loyalty programs can incentivize repeat business and reward your best customers:

- **Create a Rewards System**: Offer rewards for repeat purchases, referrals, or other actions that benefit your business. This could include discounts, free products, or exclusive offers.

- **Make It Simple**: Keep your loyalty program easy to understand and use. Complicated programs can deter customers from participating.

- **Promote Your Program**: Make sure your customers are aware of your loyalty program. Promote it through your website, social media, and email marketing.

Measuring and Improving Retention

Track and analyze customer retention metrics to gauge the effectiveness of your strategies:

- **Monitor Retention Rates**: Track how many customers return and how frequently. Analyze trends and patterns to identify areas for improvement.

- **Evaluate Customer Lifetime Value**: Calculate the average revenue generated by a customer over their lifetime. This helps you understand the impact of retention efforts on your bottom line.

- **Implement Improvement Strategies**: Based on your analysis, implement strategies to improve customer retention. This could include enhancing customer service, refining loyalty programs, or addressing common pain points.

Conclusion

Scaling up a business requires careful planning and execution. By hiring help effectively, automating processes on a budget, and focusing on customer retention, you can grow your business without jeopardizing its success. Embrace the challenges and opportunities that come with scaling, and use the strategies outlined in this chapter to build a strong foundation for sustainable growth.

As you navigate the complexities of scaling, remember that careful management and strategic planning will help you avoid common pitfalls and set your business up for long-term success. Stay adaptable, keep learning, and continue to prioritize the needs of your customers and your team. Scaling is a journey, and with the right approach, you can achieve your growth goals while maintaining control and efficiency.

Chapter 7: Navigating Setbacks with a Smile

Every entrepreneur encounters setbacks, and how you handle them can make or break your journey. This chapter explores the art of turning failures into learning experiences, the role of resilience in entrepreneurship, and knowing when to pivot your business model. By maintaining a positive attitude and using setbacks as opportunities for growth, you can continue on your path to success with confidence and humor.

Turning Failures into Funny Stories

Failure is an inevitable part of the entrepreneurial journey, but it doesn't have to be a source of despair. Instead, embracing failure with a sense of humor can provide valuable lessons and make the process less daunting.

Embracing the Humor in Failure

- **Laughing at Yourself**: One of the best ways to cope with failure is to laugh at yourself. When something goes wrong, try to find the humor in the situation. This approach can lighten the mood and reduce stress. For example, if a marketing campaign flops, joke about how it was a "creative experiment" rather than a mistake.

- **Sharing Your Stories**: Share your failures and the lessons you've learned with others. This not only helps you process your experience but also provides valuable insights to others who may be facing similar challenges. Use social media, blogs, or public speaking opportunities to tell your story in a humorous and constructive way.

- **Finding the Silver Lining**: Even in the darkest moments, there's often a silver lining. Reflect on how your failure led to unexpected opportunities or personal growth. For instance, a failed product launch might lead to a more successful pivot or a new business idea.

Case Studies of Famous Failures

- **J.K. Rowling**: Before the success of the Harry Potter series, J.K. Rowling faced numerous rejections from publishers. She famously used her experience to illustrate that persistence and belief in oneself can turn failure into triumph.

- **Steve Jobs**: Steve Jobs was ousted from Apple, the company he co-founded. Instead of letting this setback define him, he went on to build Pixar and later returned to Apple, leading it to unprecedented success. His story exemplifies how failures can lead to greater achievements.

Turning Failures into Learning Experiences

- **Analyze What Went Wrong**: Take a step back and analyze the reasons behind your failure. Was it a lack of market research, poor execution, or unforeseen external factors? Understanding the root cause will help you avoid similar mistakes in the future.

- **Adjust Your Strategy**: Use the insights gained from your failure to adjust your strategy. This might involve refining your product, changing your marketing approach, or revisiting your business plan.

- **Celebrate the Learning Process**: Instead of focusing solely on the negative aspects of failure, celebrate the learning process. Each setback brings valuable lessons that can contribute to your long-term success.

The Role of Resilience in Entrepreneurship

Resilience is a key trait for any successful entrepreneur. It's the ability to bounce back from adversity, stay motivated, and persist through challenges. Developing resilience will help you navigate the ups and downs of entrepreneurship with grace and determination.

Building Resilience

- **Develop a Growth Mindset**: Embrace challenges as opportunities for growth rather than obstacles. A growth mindset helps you see setbacks as temporary and manageable, rather than permanent failures.

- **Stay Focused on Your Goals**: Keep your long-term goals in mind and use them as motivation during difficult times. Remind yourself of why you started your business and what you hope to achieve.

- **Practice Self-Care**: Resilience is not just about mental toughness; it also involves taking care of your physical and emotional well-being. Ensure you get enough rest, exercise regularly, and maintain a healthy work-life balance.

Coping Strategies for Resilience

- **Seek Support**: Surround yourself with a supportive network of friends, family, and mentors. They can offer advice, encouragement, and a different perspective on your challenges.

- **Set Small, Achievable Goals**: Break down your larger goals into smaller, manageable tasks. Achieving these smaller goals can boost your confidence and keep you motivated.

- **Stay Adaptable**: Be open to change and willing to adapt your plans as needed. Flexibility allows you to respond effectively to unexpected challenges and opportunities.

Resilience in Action

- **Howard Schultz**: Howard Schultz faced numerous setbacks in his early career, including the failure of his first coffee venture. However, his resilience and perseverance helped him build Starbucks into a global brand.

- **Oprah Winfrey**: Oprah Winfrey overcame significant personal and professional challenges, including early career failures and personal struggles. Her resilience and determination have made her one of the most influential figures in media.

When to Pivot: Changing Your Business Model

Knowing when to pivot or change your business model is crucial for long-term success. A pivot involves making a significant change to your business strategy in response to market feedback, performance issues, or new opportunities.

Recognizing the Need for a Pivot

- **Customer Feedback**: Pay attention to customer feedback and identify patterns or recurring issues. If your customers are consistently dissatisfied with a particular aspect of your business, it may be time to reconsider your approach.

- **Market Trends**: Stay informed about market trends and changes in consumer behavior. If your current business model is becoming obsolete or less relevant, a pivot may be necessary to stay competitive.

- **Financial Performance**: Analyze your financial performance regularly. If you're consistently missing revenue targets or experiencing significant losses, it may indicate a need for a strategic change.

Types of Pivots

- **Product Pivot**: Changing your product or service offering based on market demand. For example, a company that initially focused on physical products may pivot to offering digital solutions.

- **Market Pivot**: Targeting a different customer segment or market. This could involve shifting your focus from B2B (business-to-business) to B2C (business-to-consumer) or vice versa.

- **Revenue Model Pivot**: Adjusting your revenue model or pricing strategy. This might include switching from a one-time purchase model to a subscription-based model.

Executing a Pivot Successfully

- **Conduct Thorough Research**: Before making a pivot, conduct thorough research to understand the new direction you're considering. Analyze market trends, customer needs, and competitive landscape.

- **Communicate Clearly**: Clearly communicate the reasons for the pivot to your team and stakeholders. Ensure everyone understands the new direction and how it aligns with your overall goals.

- **Monitor and Adapt**: After implementing the pivot, closely monitor its impact on your business. Be prepared to make further adjustments based on performance and feedback.

Examples of Successful Pivots

- **Netflix**: Netflix initially started as a DVD rental service but pivoted to streaming video, which became its core business. This strategic change allowed Netflix to dominate the streaming industry.

- **Slack**: Slack began as a gaming company but pivoted to a communication tool for teams after its original product failed to gain traction. This pivot led to the creation of a successful and widely used platform.

Conclusion

Navigating setbacks with a smile requires a blend of humor, resilience, and strategic thinking. By turning failures into learning experiences, building resilience, and knowing when to pivot, you can overcome challenges and continue on your path to success. Embrace the ups and downs of entrepreneurship with a positive attitude and a willingness to adapt. Remember, setbacks are not the end but opportunities for growth and improvement.

As you face challenges and setbacks, keep your sense of humor intact and use them as stepping stones towards your ultimate goals. Stay focused, stay resilient, and continue to move forward with confidence and determination. Your ability to navigate setbacks will define your journey from broke to boss, and with the right mindset, you can turn every obstacle into a triumph.

Chapter 8: Balancing Work and Life

Embarking on the journey from broke to boss is a thrilling adventure filled with challenges and opportunities. However, achieving success in business is not solely about hustling 24/7; it's also about finding a healthy balance between work and personal life. This chapter delves into the strategies for avoiding burnout, maintaining relationships while managing a demanding schedule, and finding joy in the entrepreneurial journey. By mastering these aspects, you can ensure sustainable success and personal fulfillment.

Avoiding Burnout When You're Your Own Boss

As an entrepreneur, you are often the driving force behind your business, responsible for making crucial decisions and managing day-to-day operations. This intense level of responsibility can lead to burnout if not managed properly. Avoiding burnout requires deliberate effort and self-care.

Recognizing the Signs of Burnout

- **Physical Symptoms**: Burnout can manifest as chronic fatigue, headaches, or sleep disturbances. Pay attention to your body's signals and take them seriously.

- **Emotional Symptoms**: Feelings of irritability, anxiety, or depression can indicate burnout. If you find yourself feeling emotionally drained or detached from your work, it's time to reassess your workload.

- **Behavioral Symptoms**: Decreased productivity, procrastination, and withdrawal from social interactions are common signs of burnout. If your work habits are suffering, it may be a result of burnout.

Strategies to Prevent Burnout

- **Set Boundaries**: Establish clear boundaries between work and personal time. Avoid working late into the night or on weekends. Designate specific times for work and stick to them.

- **Prioritize Self-Care**: Make self-care a priority. Engage in activities that recharge you, such as exercise, meditation, or hobbies. Ensure you get adequate rest and maintain a healthy diet.

- **Delegate Tasks**: As your business grows, delegate tasks to others. Trusting others with responsibilities can help reduce your workload and prevent burnout.

- **Take Breaks**: Regular breaks throughout the workday can improve productivity and prevent burnout. Short walks, stretching, or simply stepping away from your desk can make a big difference.

- **Seek Professional Help**: If you're struggling with burnout, consider speaking with a mental health professional. Therapy or counseling can provide support and strategies for managing stress.

Creating a Balanced Schedule

- **Time Blocking**: Use time blocking to allocate specific periods for different tasks. This approach helps you stay organized and ensures that personal time is protected.

- **Weekly Reviews**: Conduct weekly reviews to assess your workload and make adjustments as needed. Identify areas where you can delegate or streamline tasks.

- **Work-Life Integration**: Instead of striving for a strict separation between work and personal life, focus on integrating them harmoniously. Find ways to incorporate personal activities into your workday, such as taking a walk or having lunch with family.

Maintaining Relationships While Hustling Hard

Entrepreneurship often demands significant time and energy, which can impact your relationships with family, friends, and partners. Balancing work and relationships requires intentional effort and communication.

Communicating with Loved Ones

- **Set Expectations**: Clearly communicate your work commitments and schedule to your loved ones. Setting realistic expectations helps them understand your availability and reduces potential conflicts.

- **Quality Time**: Prioritize quality time with family and friends. Even if you have a busy schedule, make an effort to spend meaningful time with those you care about.

- **Be Present**: When you're with loved ones, be fully present. Avoid distractions like checking emails or taking phone calls during family time.

Involving Your Support System

- **Seek Support**: Share your entrepreneurial journey with your support system. Their encouragement and understanding can provide motivation and reduce feelings of isolation.

- **Involve Your Family**: If appropriate, involve your family in your business activities. This could include discussing business milestones or seeking their input on decisions.

- **Celebrate Together**: Celebrate achievements and milestones with your loved ones. Sharing successes reinforces the importance of their support and strengthens your relationships.

Managing Conflict

- **Address Issues Early**: If conflicts arise, address them promptly and constructively. Open communication can prevent misunderstandings and resolve issues before they escalate.

- **Seek Compromise**: Be willing to compromise and find solutions that work for both your work commitments and your relationships. Flexibility and understanding are key.

- **Professional Guidance**: If relationship issues become challenging, consider seeking guidance from a relationship counselor or therapist. Professional support can help navigate conflicts and improve communication.

Finding Joy in the Journey

The entrepreneurial journey is not just about reaching financial success; it's also about finding fulfillment and joy along the way. Embracing the process and celebrating small victories can make the journey more enjoyable and rewarding.

Cultivating a Positive Mindset

- **Focus on Progress**: Celebrate your progress and achievements, no matter how small. Recognize and appreciate the steps you've taken towards your goals.

- **Practice Gratitude**: Regularly practice gratitude by reflecting on the positive aspects of your entrepreneurial journey. Acknowledge the opportunities, experiences, and support you've received.

- **Enjoy the Process**: Embrace the ups and downs of entrepreneurship as part of the journey. Find joy in the learning process, the challenges, and the growth.

Incorporating Fun and Creativity

- **Inject Fun into Your Work**: Find ways to make your work enjoyable. This could involve adding creative elements to your tasks, celebrating milestones with your team, or incorporating hobbies into your work routine.

- **Engage in Passion Projects**: Pursue passion projects or side hobbies that bring you joy. These activities can provide a creative outlet and reduce stress.

- **Create a Positive Work Environment**: Foster a positive and supportive work environment. Encourage creativity, celebrate successes, and build strong team relationships.

Balancing Ambition and Well-Being

- **Set Realistic Goals**: Set achievable goals that align with your well-being. Avoid overloading yourself with unrealistic expectations or excessive demands.

- **Listen to Yourself**: Pay attention to your physical and emotional needs. Adjust your goals and workload based on your well-being and personal priorities.

- **Find Meaning in Your Work**: Connect with the purpose and meaning behind your entrepreneurial endeavors. Understanding the impact of your work can provide a sense of fulfillment and joy.

Examples of Finding Joy in Entrepreneurship

- **Richard Branson**: Richard Branson, founder of the Virgin Group, emphasizes the importance of having fun and enjoying the entrepreneurial journey. His approach to business includes incorporating adventure and creativity into his ventures.

- **Sara Blakely**: Sara Blakely, founder of Spanx, has spoken about the importance of maintaining a positive mindset and finding joy in the challenges of entrepreneurship. Her approach includes celebrating small wins and staying focused on her goals.

Conclusion

Balancing work and life is a crucial aspect of the entrepreneurial journey. By avoiding burnout, maintaining meaningful relationships, and finding joy in the process, you can create a fulfilling and sustainable path to success. Remember that entrepreneurship is not just about achieving financial goals but also about enjoying the journey and cultivating a balanced and rewarding life.

Embrace the challenges and triumphs of entrepreneurship with a positive mindset and a commitment to self-care and personal relationships. By finding joy in the journey and maintaining a healthy work-life balance, you can achieve long-term success and personal fulfillment.

Chapter 9: Celebrating Small Wins

In the tumultuous journey from broke to boss, the path to success can often seem long and arduous. Amidst the hustle and grind, it's crucial to pause and celebrate small wins. Recognizing and rewarding milestones not only boosts morale but also reinforces the progress you're making. This chapter explores the importance of acknowledging achievements, sharing success with humor and humility, and planning for long-term success.

Recognizing and Rewarding Milestones

The Importance of Small Wins

Small wins are critical to maintaining motivation and momentum. They serve as indicators that you are progressing towards your larger goals. Celebrating these milestones can help you stay focused and energized, even when the ultimate goal seems distant.

Identifying Small Wins

- **Achievement of Short-Term Goals**: Any goal you've set and achieved in the short term—be it a successful marketing campaign, a new client acquisition, or hitting a sales target—is a small win.

- **Overcoming Challenges**: Successfully navigating obstacles and solving problems also counts as a win. These challenges often test your resilience and creativity.

- **Positive Feedback**: Receiving positive feedback from clients, customers, or colleagues is a significant win. It validates your efforts and reinforces the value of your work.

Methods for Celebrating Small Wins

- **Personal Rewards**: Treat yourself to something special, like a day off, a nice meal, or a new gadget. Personal rewards can serve as a tangible recognition of your hard work.

- **Team Celebrations**: If you're leading a team, celebrate collective achievements. This could be through team outings, recognition awards, or public acknowledgment. Celebrating with your team fosters a positive work environment and motivates everyone.

- **Reflect and Record**: Keep a journal or log of your small wins. Regularly reviewing this record can boost your morale and provide a sense of accomplishment.

- **Share the Success**: Share your milestones with your network. Whether it's through social media, a company newsletter, or a blog, let others know about your achievements. This not only spreads positivity but also builds your reputation.

Examples of Celebrating Small Wins

- **Startup Success**: For instance, the founders of Airbnb celebrated each small milestone, from signing their first customer to reaching their first 100 users. These celebrations helped them stay motivated and focused on their long-term vision.

- **Personal Achievements**: Similarly, individuals like James Clear, author of *Atomic Habits*, emphasize the importance of celebrating small habits and improvements as part of the journey toward larger goals.

Sharing Your Success with Humor and Humility

The Role of Humor in Celebrations

Humor can play a significant role in celebrating achievements. It lightens the mood, fosters a positive atmosphere, and makes the celebration more memorable.

- **Playful Acknowledgment**: Use humor to acknowledge achievements in a fun and engaging way. For example, create a humorous "Achievement Award" for hitting a specific milestone.

- **Funny Stories**: Share anecdotes and funny stories related to the achievement. This makes the success more relatable and enjoyable for others.

- **Humorous Recognition**: Implement playful recognition methods, like a "Victory Dance" challenge where team members showcase their best dance moves to celebrate a win.

Maintaining Humility

While celebrating is important, it's equally crucial to remain humble. Humility ensures that you stay grounded and appreciative of the support you've received along the way.

- **Acknowledge Contributions**: Recognize the contributions of others who have helped you achieve your milestones. Give credit where it's due, whether it's to your team, mentors, or supporters.

- **Express Gratitude**: Share your success with a sense of gratitude. Thank those who have been part of your journey and acknowledge their role in your achievements.

- **Stay Focused on Growth**: Use celebrations as an opportunity to reflect on what you've learned and how you can continue to grow. Avoid complacency and remain focused on your long-term goals.

Examples of Humble Success Sharing

- **Entrepreneurial Stories**: Many successful entrepreneurs, like Elon Musk and Jeff Bezos, are known for their humility despite their achievements. They often highlight their teams' contributions and express gratitude for their support.

- **Public Figures**: Public figures like Malala Yousafzai emphasize humility in their success by focusing on their mission and the collective effort involved in their achievements.

Planning for Long-Term Success

Setting Future Goals

Celebrating small wins is also about planning for the future. Use your achievements as a stepping stone for setting new goals and ambitions.

- **Review and Adjust**: Regularly review your goals and adjust them based on your progress and achievements. This helps in setting realistic and attainable future objectives.

- **Strategic Planning**: Incorporate your small wins into your strategic planning. Analyze what worked well and use this information to refine your future plans.

- **Vision Expansion**: Expand your vision based on your achievements. Consider how your small wins can contribute to larger goals and long-term success.

Building on Achievements

- **Leverage Success**: Use your achievements as leverage for new opportunities. Success can open doors to partnerships, investments, or new markets.

- **Continuous Improvement**: Focus on continuous improvement. Use the momentum from your small wins to drive ongoing efforts and innovations.

- **Inspire Others**: Share your journey and achievements to inspire others. Your success story can motivate and guide others on their own entrepreneurial paths.

Examples of Long-Term Planning

- **Business Growth**: Companies like Google and Amazon have leveraged their early successes to expand their business models and enter new markets, demonstrating the importance of planning for long-term success.

- **Personal Development**: Individuals like Oprah Winfrey have used their achievements to set new goals and continue growing, illustrating how to build on success for ongoing development.

Conclusion

Celebrating small wins is an essential part of the entrepreneurial journey. By recognizing and rewarding milestones, sharing success with humor and humility, and planning for long-term success, you can maintain motivation, foster a positive environment, and continue to progress toward your goals. Remember that the path from broke to boss is not just about achieving financial success but also about enjoying and appreciating the journey along the way.

Embrace your small victories, share them with pride and humor, and use them as a foundation for future growth. By celebrating your achievements and staying focused on your long-term vision, you can create a fulfilling and successful entrepreneurial journey.

Chapter 10: Conclusion

As we approach the end of our journey from broke to boss, it's essential to reflect on the transformative process you've undergone. This concluding chapter aims to encapsulate the key takeaways from your entrepreneurial voyage, offer encouragement for future endeavors, and emphasize the importance of maintaining humor throughout your business life.

Reflecting on Your Journey from Broke to Boss

The Transformative Journey

Reflecting on your path from broke to boss involves acknowledging how far you've come and appreciating the lessons learned along the way. This journey is more than just a financial transition; it's a profound personal and professional evolution.

- **Growth and Learning**: You've learned to embrace challenges, adapt to setbacks, and seize opportunities. Each step, whether successful or not, has contributed to your growth.

- **Skill Development**: From mastering the art of door-to-door sales to building a business on a budget, you've acquired a diverse set of skills. Reflect on how these skills have shaped your entrepreneurial identity.

- **Resilience**: Your ability to bounce back from failures and navigate through tough times has strengthened your resilience. This attribute is crucial for sustaining long-term success.

Key Milestones

- **Starting Point**: Remember where you began—perhaps with little more than an idea and a lot of determination. Reflect on the initial challenges you faced and how you overcame them.

- **Significant Achievements**: Identify the key milestones you've achieved, from your first sale to scaling up your business. Celebrate these accomplishments as markers of your progress.

- **Personal Growth**: Consider how this journey has impacted you personally. How has it influenced your mindset, your relationships, and your approach to life?

Documenting Your Journey

- **Journal Entries**: Keep a journal of your experiences, reflections, and learnings. This can serve as a motivational tool and a valuable resource for future reference.

- **Success Stories**: Create a portfolio of your achievements and successes. This can be shared with others, providing inspiration and demonstrating the possibilities of perseverance.

Encouragement for Future Entrepreneurs

Embrace the Entrepreneurial Spirit

- **Continual Learning**: The entrepreneurial journey is ongoing. Embrace a mindset of continual learning and adaptability. Stay curious and open to new ideas and innovations.

- **Set New Goals**: Always set new goals to keep yourself motivated. These goals should challenge you and align with your long-term vision.

- **Seek Support**: Build a network of mentors, peers, and advisors. Their guidance and support can be invaluable as you continue to grow and evolve in your business.

Staying Motivated

- **Celebrate Achievements**: Regularly celebrate your successes, no matter how small. Acknowledging your progress keeps you motivated and focused on your goals.

- **Resilience and Adaptability**: Be prepared for setbacks and challenges. Your ability to adapt and persevere will be a critical factor in your continued success.

- **Balance and Well-Being**: Maintain a healthy work-life balance. Ensure you take time for yourself and your loved ones, as personal well-being is crucial for sustained success.

Examples of Ongoing Success

- **Successful Entrepreneurs**: Look to successful entrepreneurs like Richard Branson and Elon Musk, who continue to innovate and push boundaries despite their accomplishments. Their stories highlight the importance of continual growth and ambition.

- **Inspiring Stories**: Consider stories of individuals who have reinvented themselves and their businesses over time. Their journeys underscore the potential for ongoing success and evolution.

Keeping the Humor Alive in Your Business Life

The Role of Humor in Business

Humor is not just a tool for celebrating successes; it's a crucial element in maintaining a positive and productive work environment. It helps in navigating challenges, building relationships, and fostering creativity.

- **Lightening the Mood**: Use humor to diffuse tension and create a more enjoyable work atmosphere. It can help in managing stress and building camaraderie among your team.

- **Enhancing Creativity**: Humor can stimulate creativity and innovation. Encourage a culture where humor is appreciated and creativity is nurtured.

- **Building Relationships**: Humor is a powerful tool for building strong relationships with clients, colleagues, and customers. It makes interactions more engaging and memorable.

Incorporating Humor into Your Routine

- **Create a Fun Work Environment**: Incorporate elements of fun and humor into your workplace. This could be through themed events, humorous team challenges, or simply a culture of laughter.

- **Use Humor in Communication**: Infuse humor into your communications, whether in marketing materials, presentations, or social media. It helps to make your brand more relatable and approachable.

- **Share Your Journey**: Share your experiences and lessons learned with humor. This can be through blog posts, social media updates, or public speaking engagements. It makes your story more engaging and relatable.

Examples of Humor in Business

- **Corporate Humor**: Companies like Google and Zappos are known for their fun and engaging work environments. Their use of humor contributes to a positive culture and enhances employee satisfaction.

- **Public Figures**: Entrepreneurs like Richard Branson use humor effectively in their public personas, making their stories and brands more relatable and engaging.

Conclusion

As we conclude this journey from broke to boss, remember that success is not just about achieving financial milestones but also about personal growth, resilience, and maintaining a sense of humor. Reflect on your achievements, set new goals, and continue to embrace the entrepreneurial spirit with passion and perseverance.

Celebrate your successes, no matter how small, and share them with humor and humility. Use your experiences as a foundation for future growth and inspire others with your story. By keeping the humor alive in your business life, you'll not only enhance your own journey but also positively impact those around you.

Your path from broke to boss is a testament to your determination and hard work. As you move forward, remember that the journey is ongoing, and every challenge is an opportunity for growth. Embrace the future with confidence, enthusiasm, and a smile.

Congratulations on your journey from broke to boss. Here's to your continued success and the many achievements that lie ahead!

Don't miss out!

Visit the website below and you can sign up to receive emails whenever Michael Ferguson publishes a new book. There's no charge and no obligation.

https://books2read.com/r/B-A-CKNW-YIIUD

BOOKS 2 READ

Connecting independent readers to independent writers.